Summer SPLASH

TRAVEL
ACTIVITY BOOK

2

P9-DLZ-829

Brighter Child®
An imprint of Carson-Dellosa Publishing LLC
Greensboro, North Carolina

Brighter Child®
An imprint of Carson-Dellosa Publishing LLC
P.O. Box 35665
Greensboro, NC 27425 USA

© 2013 Carson-Dellosa Publishing LLC. Except as permitted under the United States Copyright Act, no part of this publication may be reproduced, stored, or distributed in any form or by any means (mechanically, electronically, recording, etc.) without the prior written consent of Carson-Dellosa Publishing LLC. Brighter Child® is an imprint of Carson-Dellosa Publishing LLC.

Printed in the USA • All rights reserved.
ISBN 978-1-62399-114-2

01-060131151

Table of Contents

Table of Contents

TRAVEL GAMES TIPS

Travel games are a great way to break up the boredom of a long distance trip. Guessing games, word games, and category games provide hours of fun and learning. Use this section to help you plan ahead to get even more fun out of your travels!

Portable Fun Pak

Before your trip, gather together a "fun pak"—a set of things that will help you occupy your time while traveling. Choose items that are small and portable. Place them in a backpack or a tote bag.

Skim through the ideas in this book and mark the games you think you'd like to play on your trip. Some games require you to prepare something before your trip. Be sure to include any materials needed for those activities in your fun pak.

What and how much you take will depend on how long you plan to travel. Also, some things that are appropriate for one form of travel may not be ideal for another.

ALPHABET GAMES

By the second grade, your child has mastered the ABCs, but now he or she will be diving into alphabetical order! In this section, you'll find fun games that will allow your child to practice the alphabet, and—better yet!—keep him or her from getting bored!

Alphabet Soup

In this game, players try to be the first to "drink" their alphabet soup.

Each player needs a pencil and a sheet of paper. Each player draws a large circle on his or her paper to represent a soup bowl. Inside the bowl, each player writes 12 letters. Now, everyone's ready to begin the game!

As you travel, look for signs that contain the letters in your soup bowl. If you spot a letter, call it out and cross it off your sheet of paper. Each sign is good for only one player and one letter. The first player to cross off all the letters has finished "drinking" the alphabet soup and is the winner.

Say It Backward

Can you say the alphabet backward without making a mistake? That's the challenge in this game. Each person can try individually or one player can say **Z**, the next **Y**, the following person **X**, and so on.

For an extra challenge, try singing the alphabet backward to the tune of the alphabet song.

WOW!

Tricky Tongue Twisters

Give your tongue a workout with this game!

Make up a sentence in which every word begins with **A**, such as "Alan asked Adam about ants." Then, say the sentence three times fast and challenge others to do the same. Everyone who successfully says the sentence gets a point.

The game continues with another player making up a sentence for **B**. The winner is the person with the most points.

I SELL SEASHELLS BY THE SEASHORE!

SUSIE'S SHELLS

NUMBER GAMES

At the end of their second grade year, children should be able to fluently add and subtract within 100, and will be delving into beginning multiplication. There are plenty of ways for your child to practice math while you're on the go—you just need to know where to look!

Number Lotto

Use the lotto gameboards below and on pages 13 and 14. Have each player write a number from **0** to **20** in the 16 sections. Next, have everyone try to spot the numbers that are on his or her gameboard. The first person to spot a number calls it out and crosses it off his or her gameboard.

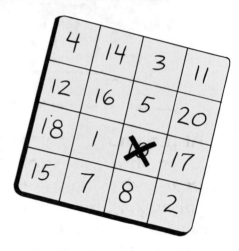

Players who have that same number do not cross it off their gameboards; only the first person to spot the number gets to cross it off. The player who crosses off the most numbers is the winner.

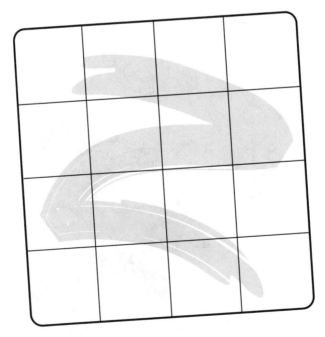

Number Lotto

(Directions are found on page 12.)

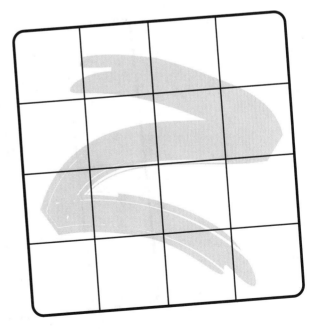

Number Lotto

(Directions are found on page 12.)

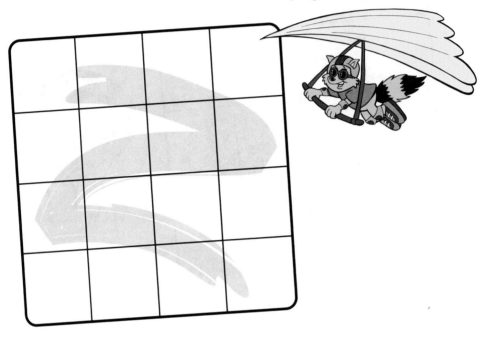

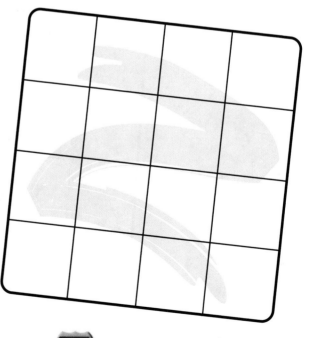

FABULOUS WORD SEARCH PUZZLES

Word search puzzles encourage children to use problem solving and creative thinking skills to recognize words hidden in the puzzle. It also provides children with excellent practice in spelling and defining common words.

Look What I See!

Find and circle the words in the puzzle.

```
d  b  u  m  w  i  a  y
o  d  l  u  e  m  w  o
w  a  i  s  n  l  a  u
n  f  t  a  t  o  y  b
a  t  t  i  e  o  c  i
m  e  l  d  m  k  a  g
y  r  e  o  e  s  n  r
```

down	after	away	big
little	said	went	my
look	you	me	can

How High Can We Go?

Find and circle the words in the puzzle.

f	i	n	d	l	d	
h	t	r	e	y	p	u	f
e	w	u	z	o	l	f	o
r	o	n	d	u	a	u	r
e	c	o	m	e	y	n	w
s	k	m	a	k	e	n	e
o	j	u	m	p	p	y	o
e	h	e	l	p	a	

here	come		
find	funny	for	jump
two	you	so	help
we	make	play	run

Ticket, Please!

Find and circle the words in the puzzle.

```
a  l  m  j  e  f  o  p  q  d  g  u  i
c  f  h  i  k  f  f  c  e  b  m  n  p
b  e  r  t  y  s  e  v  e  n  z  c  b
h  o  e  r  s  j  t  e  n  l  h  n  g
u  x  e  t  c  d  o  n  e  t  h  i  k
w  f  l  n  y  x  f  e  z  h  d  i  o
p  i  e  i  s  t  o  i  e  r  a  u  p
d  v  v  n  i  w  u  g  r  e  n  k  l
a  e  e  e  x  o  r  h  o  e  d  f  h
b  c  n  d  f  g  i  t  j  l  m  n  o
```

TICKET

zero   four   eight
one   five   nine
two   six   ten
three   seven   eleven

Heading for the Slopes

Find and circle the words in the puzzle.

```
g i o w t r z u y
s s s s s s t o p r t
a h h h h h t r o e c s v p
c o i o a a b e p r w n m x
y u r u r l l t z e m a n d
g l l t t e l s h e l l o s h
r o d s s s o s h a r p h h s
s h s h o w w s h e e p s o h
s h o r t s h a p e s h i n e
```

shell	should	shape
shouts	sheep	sharp
she	short	shirts
shine	shallow	show
	shares	

Creative Colors

Find and circle the words in the puzzle.

```
o r a n g e b d c a e g i k r z t
p x h o e b u n w n f a d f e q x
i l m n b l v c x z a s f g d h a
n y u i o u r e w q t p w h i t e
k g r a y e x p b n v m x k y u p
b u d r u g t u b r o w n m e n o
l a s d m r r r v n e t y w l l h
a b d f g e h p j k m u z m l n e
c g h k o e i l e w n l v f o g n
k s d u e n l e j o m c s x w y w
```

yellow
red   gray
blue   orange   pink
black   green   white
brown   purple

A Gentle Breeze

Find and circle the words in the puzzle.

grin	yell
shut	street
fast	unhappy
steps	beautiful
starts	go
cap	talk
same	small

```
t w p x m a u o s g r a t a k g a
n s r e p g h b a a r v r h i o l
v w b n s f p r m d u i d t e f m
b o t m f d g i e n h r n p o q c
a b z p c i e s s k c f h c t m e
j l t e a y m i m u q w b o a l t
e g f d r t u s a s t a r t s p l
h r y c f m o t l w f y e b h j e
k j p g i e q a l s o f m l p n i
s h u t b e a u t i f u l y e l l
f a s t s t r e e t u n h a p p y
c m a s t e p s t a l k g o g a t
```

A Refreshing Dip

Find and circle the words in the puzzle.

```
e  m  w  a  t  e  r  s  i  q  t  a  s  t
t  s  c  l  e  a  r  w  e  a  q  c  j  a
a  b  u  b  b  l  e  s  i  u  a  y  x  c
b  r  e  a  t  h  e  l  a  l  o  p  d  h
r  o  c  k  s  c  a  r  e  f  n  o  e  u
p  l  a  n  t  s  i  s  e  e  i  p  n  m
x  a  i  r  f  u  n  i  l  y  a  n  t  o
b  c  p  u  m  p  s  e  r  w  e  t  s  j
y  i  d  s  w  i  m  u  i  o  g  h  r  k
t  e  f  t  g  i  l  l  j  m  h  i  o  x
```

eat	fins
clear	breathe
pumps	scales
eye	aquariums
fun	plants
bubbles	water
gill	air
swim	tail
care	rocks

FUN WITH LICENSE PLATES

While traveling, your child may have the opportunity to see different states or countries than he or she has ever seen before. Playing games with license plates is a great way to encourage an interest in travel, in your country, and in the world.

FUN4U

Number Combinations

In this game, only the numbers on license plates count. The first player writes the license plate number of the first car, the second player writes the number of the second car, and so on. When everyone has had a turn, each player tallies his or her combinations according to the chart below. Play the game several times. The person with the highest score wins.

One Pair
(two numbers that are the same)
— **1 point**

Two Pairs
(two sets of like numbers)
— **2 points**

Three of a Kind
(three numbers that are the same)
— **3 points**

Four of a Kind
(four numbers that are the same)
— **4 points**

Three or More in a Row (three or more numbers in sequence, such as 4, 5, 6)
— **5 points**

MLP 224
COLORADO

License Plate Lotto

Use the lotto gameboards below and on pages 26–28. Each player fills in the 25 sections with numbers from **1** to **9** and letters of the alphabet. The numbers and letters may be used more than once.

Next, one player calls out a number or a letter from the license plate of a passing vehicle. Players with the corresponding number or letter cross it off their gameboard. The game continues with different players calling out numbers or letters. The first player to cross off all the letters or numbers on his or her lotto gameboard wins.

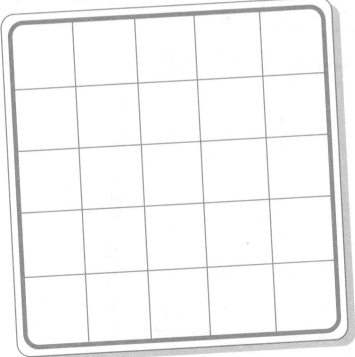

License Plate Lotto

(Directions are found on page 25.)

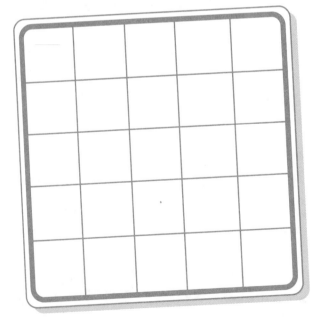

License Plate Lotto

(Directions are found on page 25.)

License Plate Lotto

(Directions are found on page 25.)

CAN YOU SPOT THAT?

Observation is the first step in forming critical thinking skills. It is important to encourage your second grader to observe things around him or her, which gives your child practice in the important skills of classifying and identifying basic sight words.

Food Fun

Use the Food Fun lists below and on pages 31 and 32. See how many food words or pictures of food you can find while traveling. Look for them on billboards, restaurant signs, and other sources. See how many items you can spot in 30 minutes.

FOOD FUN LIST

_____

_____

_____

_____

_____

_____

_____

FOOD FUN LIST

_____

_____

_____

_____

_____

_____

_____

Food Fun

(Directions are found on page 30.)

FOOD FUN LIST

_____
_____
_____
_____
_____
_____
_____
_____
_____
_____
_____
_____
_____
_____

FOOD FUN LIST

_____
_____
_____
_____
_____
_____
_____
_____
_____
_____
_____
_____
_____
_____

Food Fun

(Directions are found on page 30.)

FOOD FUN LIST

_____

_____

_____

_____

_____

_____

_____

_____

_____

_____

_____

FOOD FUN LIST

_____

_____

_____

_____

_____

_____

_____

_____

_____

_____

_____

Traveler's Tic Tac Toe

This game requires two players sitting next to each other. One person is **X** and the other is **O**.

Use the grids below and on pages 34–36. Write in each section the name of something you might see during your travels, such as a stop sign or

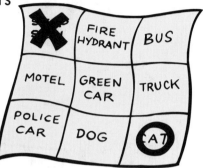

a fire hydrant. The first player to see one of the items calls it out and writes his or her designated letter in the corresponding place on the grid. The first person to get three in a row wins.

Traveler's Tic Tac Toe

(Directions are found on page 33.)

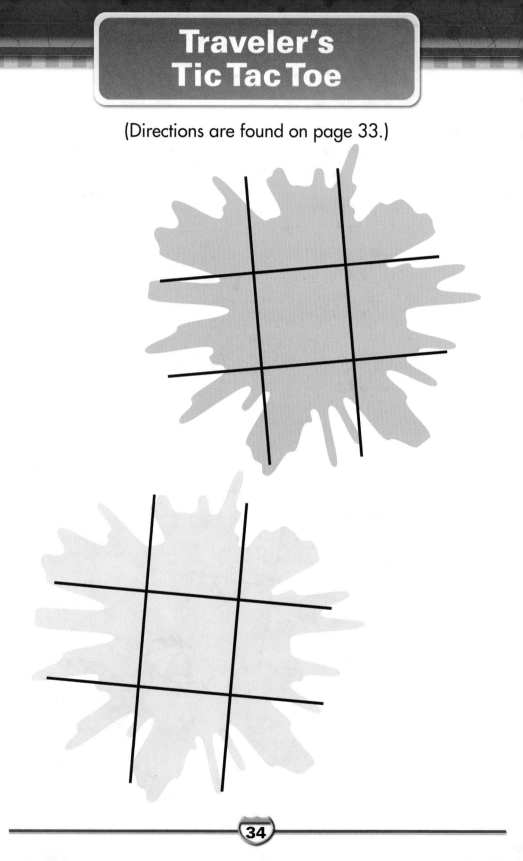

Traveler's Tic Tac Toe

(Directions are found on page 33.)

Traveler's Tic Tac Toe

(Directions are found on page 33.)

Traveler's Scavenger Hunt

Here's a fun scavenger hunt that everyone in the car will enjoy playing.

Together, make a list of 12 or more things you will most likely see on your trip. The list can include general things, such as a billboard or a farm, and very specific items, such as a black-and-white cow or a sign that displays the letter **Z**.

While traveling, everyone helps look for the things on the list. The first person to spot an item calls it out, then writes his or her initial beside that item on the list. If two people call out an item at the same time, both their initials are written down. The goal is to find as many things on the list as possible within a given amount of time or before the trip is over. (Lists are found on pages 38–40.)

Traveler's Scavenger Hunt

(Directions are found on page 37.)

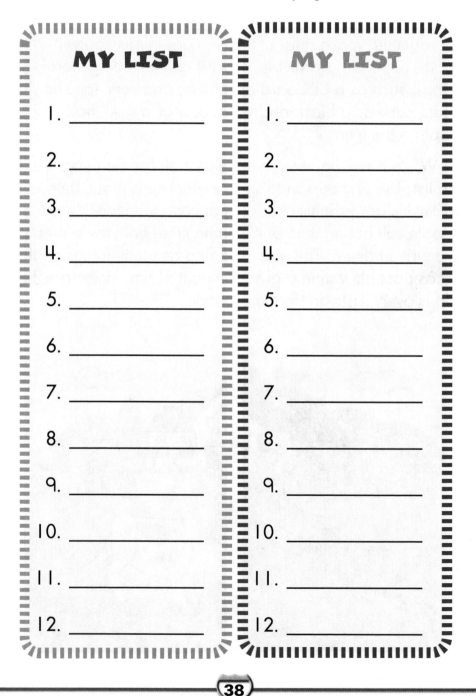

MY LIST	MY LIST
1. _____	1. _____
2. _____	2. _____
3. _____	3. _____
4. _____	4. _____
5. _____	5. _____
6. _____	6. _____
7. _____	7. _____
8. _____	8. _____
9. _____	9. _____
10. _____	10. _____
11. _____	11. _____
12. _____	12. _____

Traveler's Scavenger Hunt

(Directions are found on page 37.)

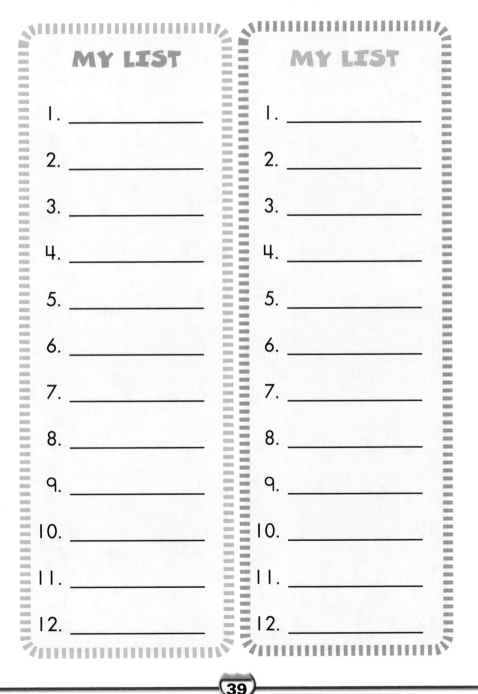

MY LIST

1. _____
2. _____
3. _____
4. _____
5. _____
6. _____
7. _____
8. _____
9. _____
10. _____
11. _____
12. _____

MY LIST

1. _____
2. _____
3. _____
4. _____
5. _____
6. _____
7. _____
8. _____
9. _____
10. _____
11. _____
12. _____

Traveler's Scavenger Hunt

(Directions are found on page 37.)

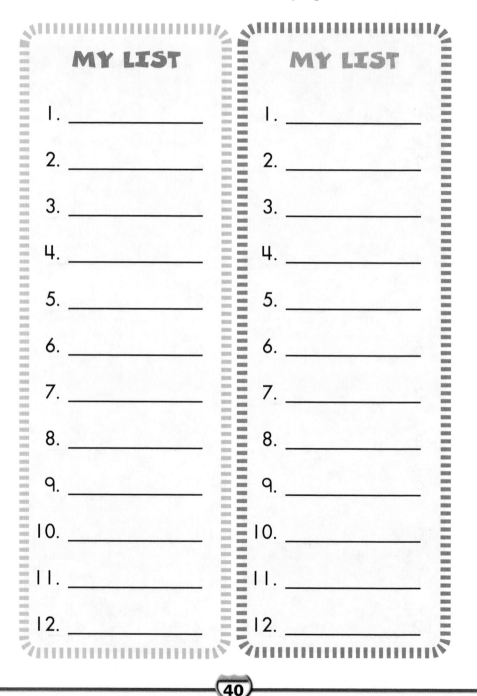

MY LIST

1. _____
2. _____
3. _____
4. _____
5. _____
6. _____
7. _____
8. _____
9. _____
10. _____
11. _____
12. _____

MY LIST

1. _____
2. _____
3. _____
4. _____
5. _____
6. _____
7. _____
8. _____
9. _____
10. _____
11. _____
12. _____

Roadside Bingo

Use the bingo cards below and on pages 42–44. Players fill in the sections with various things they might see on their trip, such as a black cat, a flagpole, a white van, and a fire hydrant. When players see one of the items on their bingo card, they cross it off. The first person to make a straight line vertically, horizontally, or diagonally calls out "Bingo!" and wins.

Roadside Bingo

(Directions are found on page 41.)

B I N G O

Roadside Bingo

(Directions are found on page 41.)

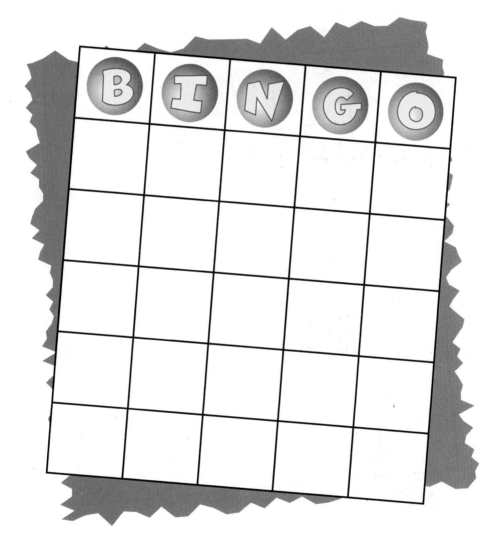

Roadside Bingo

(Directions are found on page 41.)

B	I	N	G	O

44

My Favorite Color

Each player writes the name of his or her favorite color on a sheet of paper. Then, players see how many things of their color they can find. When an appropriate object is spotted, the player calls it out and writes it on his or her list.

One type of object counts for 1 point. For example, if a player's color is red and three red cars are spotted, only 1 point is scored. If two players have the same color, the player who spots the object first and calls it out earns the point. Set a time limit, and see who can find the greatest number of objects for his or her color.

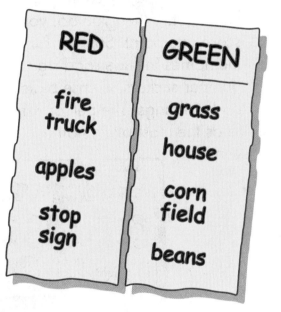

RED	GREEN
fire truck	grass
apples	house
stop sign	corn field
	beans

City, State, and Country

Be the first to spot the name of a city, state, or country and call it out. When you do, you score one point. Sources for the names include road signs, bumper stickers, license plates, and buildings. The person who finds the most place names wins.

WELCOME TO COLUMBUS OHIO

525·AFP
IOWA

FOLLOWING DIRECTIONS & READING MAPS

Maps are an important part of everyday life. Your second grader will begin to become familiar and gain confidence with maps by exploring familiar places.

Old-Time Stagecoach Ride

Follow the horseshoe trail to tour the old western town. Write the names of the places in the order they are passed along the trail. Remember, the ride starts and ends at the same place.

1. _____
2. _____
3. _____
4. _____
5. _____
6. _____
7. _____
8. _____
9. _____
10. _____

Helping a Lost Student

Recess is over. A second-grade student cannot find her way to Room 1. Can you help her? Look at the map. The dotted line shows the way from the playground to Room 1.

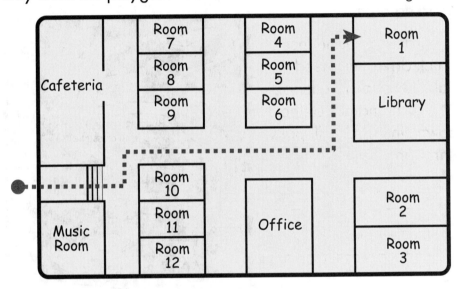

Number the directions by following the path of the dotted line.

_____ Turn north at the bottom of the steps.

_____ First, you open the door and come into the school.

_____ Continue walking down the long hall past the office.

_____ Turn north when you reach the library.

_____ Walk by the music room.

_____ Keep walking until you come to Room 1.

_____ Go down three steps.

_____ Turn east and walk down the hall between Rooms 9 and 10.

A truck driver has to decide which roads he will use to deliver his cargo to the depot. He has to be sure his truck will go under the bridges and through the tunnels. His truck is 12 feet high. The heights of the bridges and tunnels are marked on the map.

Trace the route the truck driver will need to take to reach the depot. Write the names of the towns the truck will pass through in order.

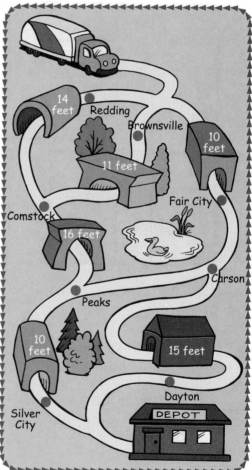

1. _____

2. _____

3. _____

4. _____

5. _____

REBUS PUZZLES

Children learn best when they are interested in what they are learning. These entertaining puzzles will excite your child and, in turn, he or she will learn more effectively.

ANSWER:

ANSWER:

Fairy Tale Villain

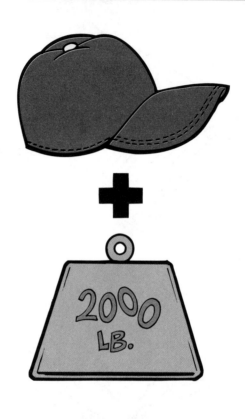

ANSWER:

A Southern State

ANSWER:

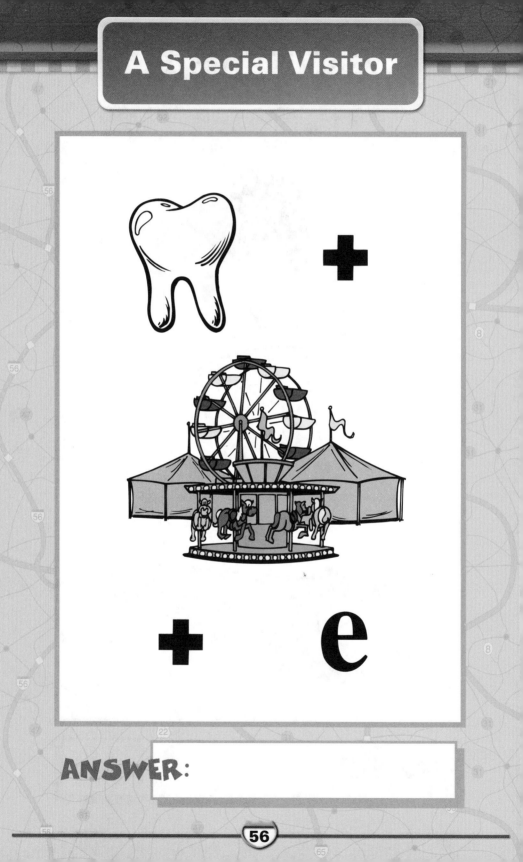

ANSWER:

CATEGORY GAMES

Movies? Colors? Animals? There's no end to the types of categories you can choose for these games. Naming objects that belong in different categories will help your child master the important skills of sorting and classifying.

Movie Trivia

Do you like movies? Then, this category game is just for you!

One person begins by naming a movie. Then, each player takes a turn naming a character or an actor from the movie. Everyone helps to collect as many names as possible.

Variation: Play this game with two teams, and have each team write down the names on a sheet of paper. The team with the longest list wins.

Word Pyramids

Use the pyramid below and on pages 60–62.

To begin this game one player names a general category, such as animals or action words. The players then have to fill in their pyramids with names of animals or action words. The top row will have a two-letter word, the second row will have a three-letter word, and so on. The first person to finish the pyramid wins the game.

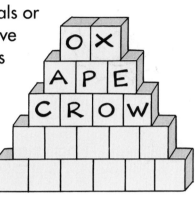

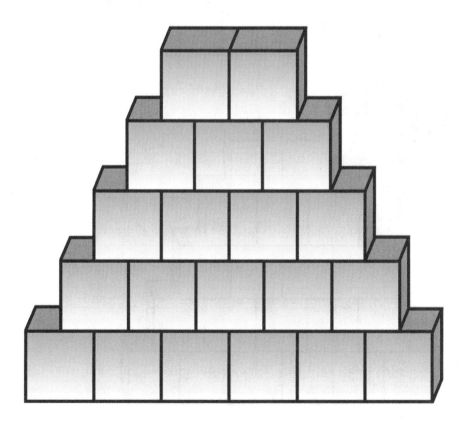

Word Pyramids

(Directions are found on page 59.)

Word Pyramids

(Directions are found on page 59.)

Word Pyramids

(Directions are found on page 59.)

What's In a Name?

Use the grids on pages 64 and 65. Write the name of a family member vertically on the grid. Then, write three categories at the top. (Examples: city, food, animal.) Next, write down items that fit the three categories and begin with the letters of the person's name. See how long it takes you to complete the sheet.

This game can be played with people working together or individually.

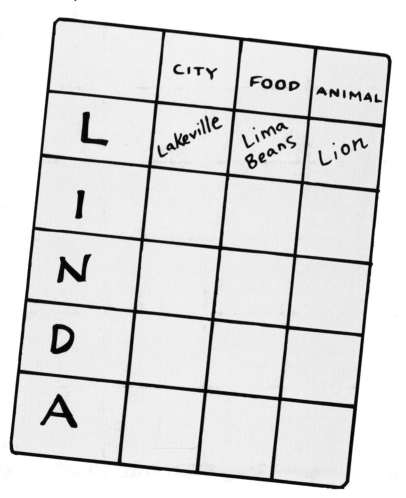

	CITY	FOOD	ANIMAL
L	Lakeville	Lima Beans	Lion
I			
N			
D			
A			

What's In a Name?

(Directions are found on page 63.)

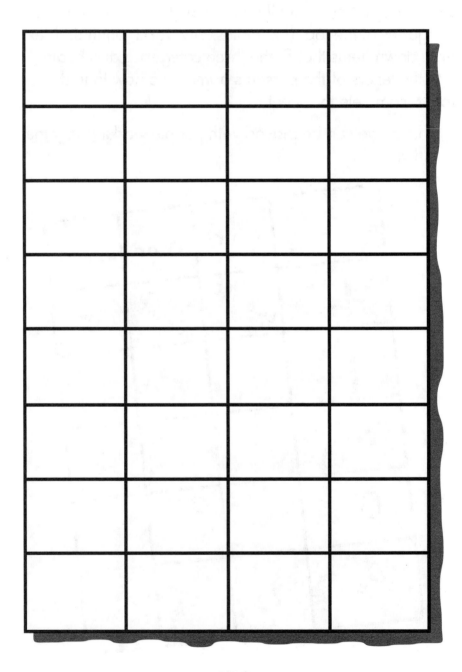

What's In a Name?

(Directions are found on page 63.)

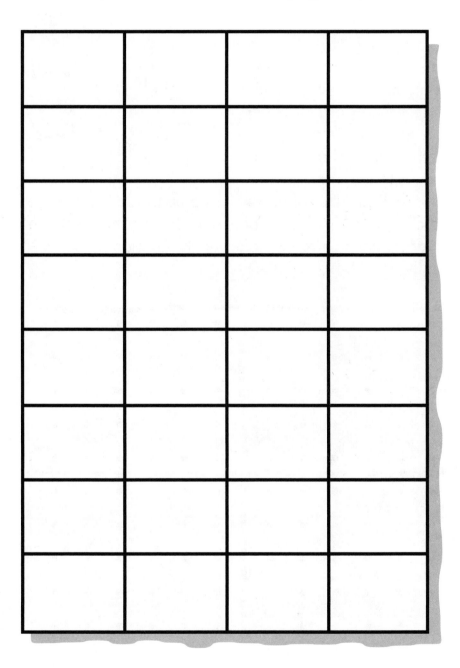

Boxed In

Use the gameboards on this page and on pages 67 and 68.

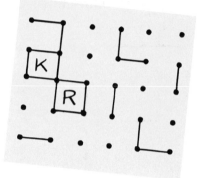

Two people can play this strategy game. Each player takes a turn drawing a line to connect a pair of dots either horizontally or vertically. When a line is drawn so that a box is made, that player writes the first letter of his or her name inside the box and claims it. After all the dots have been connected, the players count how many boxes each has made. The one with the most boxes wins.

Boxed In

(Directions are found on page 66.)

Boxed In

(Directions are found on page 66.)

INCREDIBLE CROSSWORD PUZZLES

Crossword puzzles will help build your child's vocabulary, critical thinking skills, and spelling. Completing these puzzles will also help your child improve reading skills!

Astro Adventure

Use the Word Bank to help you find words that match the pictures. Then, write them in the puzzle.

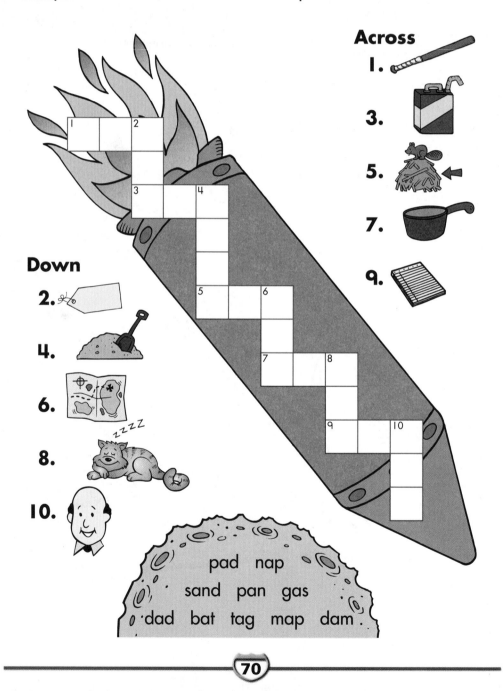

Across

1.

3.

5.

7.

9.

Down

2.

4.

6.

8.

10.

pad nap
sand pan gas
dad bat tag map dam

Umbrellas Up!

Use the Word Bank to help you find words that match the pictures. Then, write them in the puzzle.

Across

1.
3.
5.
7.
9.

Down

2.
4.
5.
6.
8.
10.

mug   bus   sun   pup   hut
gum   hump   bug   sub   plum
nuts

Don't Just Sit There!

Use the Word Bank to help you find words that match the pictures. Then, write them in the puzzle.

Across

3. 10¢   7.

4.   8.

6.

Word Bank:
dinner   dime   desk
dock   dust   donkey
deer   dent   down
drum   dress

Down

1.   2.   3.

4.   5.   7.

Hit the Hay!

Use the Word Bank to help you find words that match the pictures. Then, write them in the puzzle.

Across

1.
6.
3.
7.
4.
5.

Word Bank:

hop   hole
hill   happy
helmet   hen
hose   hut   hay
hand   hat
hammer

Down

1.
2.
3.
4.
6.
7.

Climbing Koala

Use the Word Bank to help you find words that match the pictures. Then, write them in the puzzle.

Across

1.

3.

4.

6.

7.

Down

1.

2.

3.

4.

5.

king   keys   kettle
kangaroo   kits
koala bear   kick
kitten   kind   kite

Is It Really Magic?

Use the Word Bank to help you find words that match the pictures. Then, write them in the puzzle.

Across

1.

2.

3.

5.

7.   8.

Down

1.   4.

2.   6.

3.   7.

mittens   melt
map   mitt
mug   mop
mail   moon
mask   match
monster   mouse

Nap Time in the Nest

Use the Word Bank to help you find words that match the pictures. Then, write them in the puzzle.

Across

2.

4.

5.

6.

Down

1.

2. 1, 2, 3, 4, ...

3.

5.

6.

note nose numbers
needle net nail nine
nurse nest

Ready Your Robot

Use the Word Bank to help you find words that match the pictures. Then, write them in the puzzle.

Across

2.

4.

5.

6.

7.

Down

1.

2.

3.

4.

5.

rope
road
robe
race
rake
raft
raindrop
ribbon
rabbit
read

Veggie Delight

Use the Word Bank to help you find words that match the pictures. Then, write them in the puzzle.

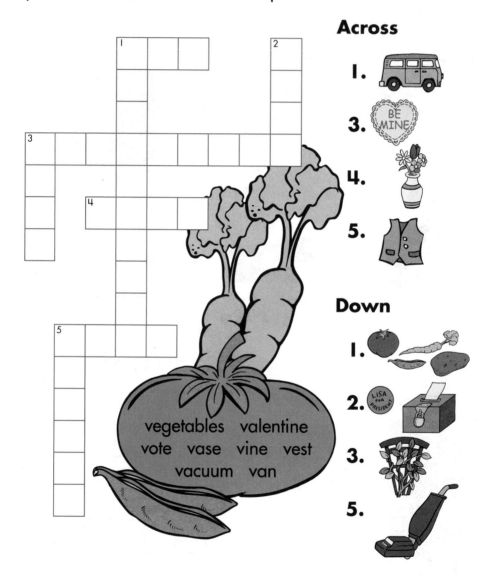

Across

1.

3. BE MINE

4.

5.

Down

1.

2. LISA FOR PRESIDENT

3.

5.

vegetables   valentine
vote   vase   vine   vest
vacuum   van

TAKE A GUESS

These guessing games will challenge your child by encouraging critical thinking. In order to guess the correct answer, your child must observe and decipher the information he or she has while making deductions to find the correct answer.

In the Doghouse

Stay out of the doghouse!

Use the spaces on pages 81 and 82, or use another sheet of paper.

Player A begins by thinking of a word or name (at least 7 letters long). Here are some examples: an action word or famous person.

Player A draws the number of blanks needed for the answer.

The other players take turns guessing the letters. Player A writes the correct letter guesses in the correct blanks. An incorrect guess means a part (wall, wall, floor, ceiling, side of roof, side of roof, and door) of the doghouse will be drawn. The last person to guess incorrectly and not guess the answer will have his or her name written on the doghouse sign.

The person who guesses the word or name correctly is the next person to think of a word or name.

In the Doghouse

(Directions are found on page 80.)

In the Doghouse

(Directions are found on page 80.)

Twenty Questions

One player starts the game by thinking of a person, place, or thing. Then, the other players take turns asking questions that can be answered by "yes" or "no." (Examples: Are you thinking of a person? Is the person a movie star?) You can keep asking questions until someone makes a correct guess or until you've reached 20 questions.

Players who think they have the answer can make a guess when it's their turn. A player who makes an incorrect guess is out. The player who guesses correctly gets to think of the next person, place, or thing.

Famous Initials

This game is a variation of "Twenty Questions." Player A gives the initials of a famous person such as a historical figure, a movie star, or an author. The other players then have to guess who that person is by asking questions that can be answered by "yes" or "no." If a person guesses the correct answer, he or she gets to think of a new set of initials. If no correct guesses are made before 20 questions are asked, Player A gets to think of another celebrity.

WORD CHALLENGE GAMES

Whether it's thinking of words with double meanings or pairing objects together, your child will be forced to think on his or her feet, therefore improving concentration. Just watch your child's imagination expand!

Add It Up

In this game, someone chooses a category, such as animals, food, or colors. Each player then writes a word that fits the category. Everyone adds up his or her points according to the values of the letters in the word. (Use page 87 to help you score this game.) The person with the most points wins.

Be careful—the longest word isn't necessarily the one that will score the most points. For example, **cheetah** scores 50 points but **skunk** scores 76 points.

Add It Up

(Directions are found on page 86.)

A=1 B=2 C=3 D=4

E=5 F=6 G=7 H=8 I=9

J=10 K=11 L=12 M=13 N=14

O=15 P=16 Q=17 R=18 S=19

T=20 U=21 V=22 W=23

X=24 Y=25 Z=26

Double-Duty Names

To play the game, players have to write down people's names that can also mean something else. (Examples: Rose, Penny, Pat, Mark, Grant, Bill.) Players can work individually or as a group to make a list as long as possible.

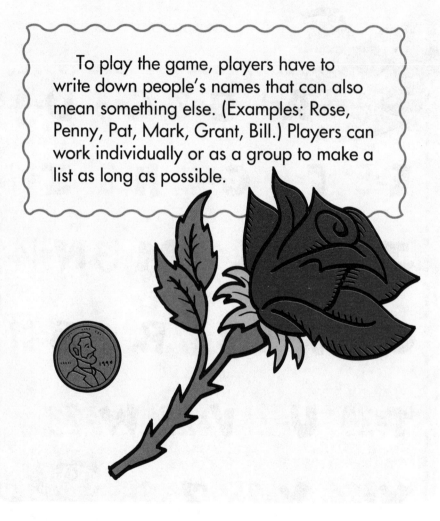

Salt and Pepper

In this game, players list names of people or objects that are usually paired together. After 5 minutes, the person with the greatest number of pairs wins. Here are some ideas:

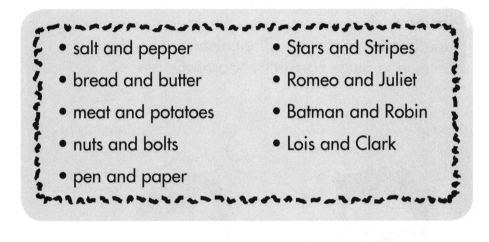

- salt and pepper
- bread and butter
- meat and potatoes
- nuts and bolts
- pen and paper
- Stars and Stripes
- Romeo and Juliet
- Batman and Robin
- Lois and Clark

What Am I Spelling?

Player A thinks of a word and gives the first letter. The other players then guess what the word is. Player A gives the second letter and the other players guess. The game continues with the word being spelled one letter at a time and a guess being made after each letter. The person who is the first person to guess correctly chooses the next word.

ANSWER KEY

Word search:

```
e m w a t e r   s i a t a s t
t s c l e a r w e a q c j a
a a b u b b l e s i u a c x c h
b r e a t h e l l a y o d u m
r o c k s c a r e f n p e h o
p l a n t s i s e i n o j
x a i r f u n i i y e t i o k
b c p u m p s e r i p a n r o h
y i d s w i m u r w t g x
t e f t g i l l j m h i o
```

Crossword answers:

bat
gas
sand
dam
pan
pad
dad

Word bank: pad nap sand pan gas dad bat tag map dam

Across
1.
3.
5.
7.
9.

Down
2.
4.
6.
8.
10.

ANSWER: step

Answer Key

16

17

18

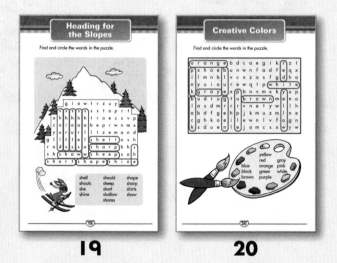

19

20

Answer Key

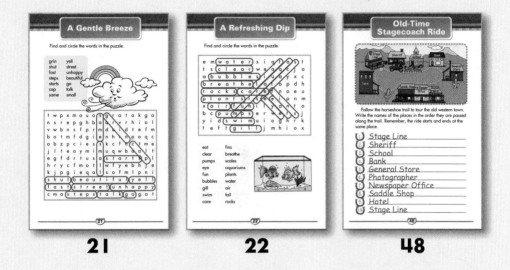

21

22

48

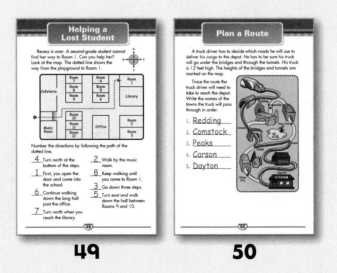

Helping a Lost Student

Recess is over. A second-grade student cannot find her way to Room 1. Can you help her? Look at the map. The dotted line shows the way from the playground to Room 1.

Number the directions by following the path of the dotted line.

__4__ Turn north at the bottom of the steps.

__1__ First, you open the door and come into the school.

__6__ Continue walking down the long hall past the office.

__7__ Turn north when you reach the library.

__2__ Walk by the music room.

__8__ Keep walking until you come to Room 1.

__3__ Go down three steps.

__5__ Turn east and walk down the hall between Rooms 9 and 10.

49

Plan a Route

A truck driver has to decide which roads he will use to deliver his cargo to the depot. He has to be sure his truck will go under the bridges and through the tunnels. His truck is 12 feet high. The heights of the bridges and tunnels are marked on the map.

Trace the route the truck driver will need to take to reach the depot. Write the names of the towns the truck will pass through in order.

1. Redding
2. Comstock
3. Peaks
4. Carson
5. Dayton

50

Answer Key

Family Member

ANSWER: stepmother

52

An Early Route

ANSWER: paper boy

53

Fairy Tale Villain

ANSWER: Captain Hook

54

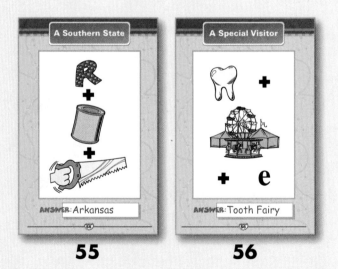

A Southern State

ANSWER: Arkansas

55

A Special Visitor

ANSWER: Tooth Fairy

56

Answer Key

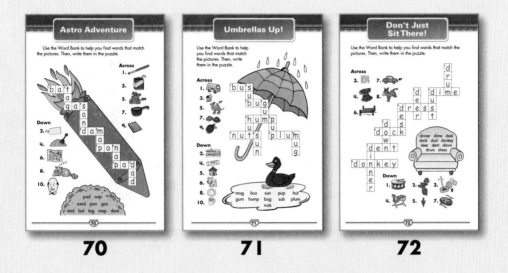

70 **71** **72**

73 **74**

Answer Key

Is It Really Magic?

Use the Word Bank to help you find words that match the pictures. Then, write them in the puzzle.

Across
1. mail
2. match
3. mop
4. monster
5. mask
7.
8. mittens
mug

Down
1.
2.
3.
4.
5.
6.
7.

mouse

Word Bank: mittens, melt, mop, mitt, mug, mop, mail, moon, mask, match, monster, mouse

75

Nap Time in the Nest

Use the Word Bank to help you find words that match the pictures. Then, write them in the puzzle.

Across
2. nail
4. note
5. needle
6. nine
numbers
nest

Down
1.
2.
3.
4.
5.
6.

nurse

Word Bank: note, nose, numbers, needle, net, nail, nine, nurse, nest

76

Ready Your Robot

Use the Word Bank to help you find words that match the pictures. Then, write them in the puzzle.

Across   **Down**
2.   1.
4.   2.
5.   3.
6.   4.
7.   5. robe
                 rabbit
                 read   raft
                 race
                 rope

Word Bank: rope, road, robe, race, rake, raft, raindrop, ribbon, rabbit, read

77

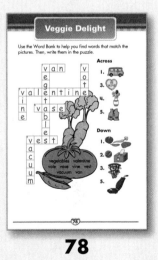

Veggie Delight

Use the Word Bank to help you find words that match the pictures. Then, write them in the puzzle.

Across
van   vote
valentine
vine   vase
vest
vacuum

Down
1.
2.
3.
4.
5.

Word Bank: vegetables, valentine, vote, vase, vine, vest, vacuum, van

78

96